Greatest Forgiveness

Greatest Forgiveness

*Bring Joy and Peace to
Your Life with the Power of
Unconditional Forgiveness*

Dr. and Master
Zhi Gang Sha
with
**Master Cynthia Deveraux
and Master David Lusch**

BenBella Books, Inc.
Dallas, TX

Copyright © 2019 Heaven's Library Publication Corp.
heavenslibrary@drsha.com

BenBella Books, Inc.
10440 N. Central Expressway, Suite 800
Dallas, TX 75231
www.benbellabooks.com
Send feedback to feedback@benbellabooks.com.

"Heaven's Library," "Heart and Soul Series," and Heaven's Library lotus logo are trademarks of Heaven's Library Publication Corp.

Printed in the United States of America
10 9 8 7 6 5 4 3 2 1

Library of Congress Cataloging-in-Publication Data
is available upon request.
ISBN 9781946885760 (trade cloth)
e-ISBN 9781946885753 (electronic)

Editing by Leah Wilson
Copyediting by Stacia Seaman
Text composition by Aaron Edmiston
Proofreading by Michael Fedison
Cover design by Henderson Ong
Printed by Lake Book Manufacturing

Distributed to the trade by Two Rivers Distribution, an Ingram brand
www.tworiversdistribution.com

Special discounts for bulk sales (minimum of 25 copies) are available.
Please contact bulkorders@benbellabooks.com.

Contents

v

List of Figures

Introduction

EVERY HUMAN BEING has challenges in life. These challenges could be in health, relationships, finances, business, or the spiritual journey, which is the enlightenment journey for the soul, heart, mind, and body.

A key to life is how one deals with its challenges. Some people face their challenges seriously and learn the lessons the challenges bring. Some people become depressed and lose hope. Some people become very upset, even angry, and choose to fight with their challenges, whether they are in health, relationships, or business.

My personal belief is that when you face challenges in life, it is most important to understand the root cause of the challenges. Then learn how to remove the root cause. This can not only transform the challenge but also prevent it from recurring.

In this small book, I will explain clearly why forgiveness is the vital practice to remove the root causes of all kinds of life challenges. I will give you a powerful tool, Tao Calligraphy, to boost your practice of forgiveness.

First, I want to share some of the effects of not forgiving.

We can be unforgiving because we have been hurt very badly, perhaps even cruelly. We can be unforgiving because we perceive some injustice. We can be unforgiving because of a sense of righteousness. We can be unforgiving because we feel something has been stolen from us—physically, emotionally, mentally, financially, or in a relationship. There are many reasons why it can be difficult to forgive.

Think about how it feels when you are not able to forgive. You could hang on to resentment, even great anger and thoughts of revenge. You could hold great fear and anxiety about the one who has harmed you.

Think about how it feels when you cannot be forgiven for some harm you have caused. You could have guilt, shame, a loss of some beautiful aspect of your life, and more.

If you have had any of these experiences, you know it does not feel good. When you cannot forgive someone you feel has hurt you, you could suffer more in your emotions, health, relationships, finances, and other aspects of your life.

There are many heart-touching stories of forgiveness in this book. They demonstrate the transformation that can occur when one is able to let go and forgive. Research studies have shown that forgiveness reduces stress and can transform health. If we cannot forgive and are bound by our resentment, bitterness, desire for revenge, and more, it is we who suffer. When we stay stuck in our pain and negativity, we can very easily create even more negativity through our thoughts and words. This could bring even greater negativity to our lives: isolation, hatred, disharmony, and more.

There is an ancient saying:

**Before you embark on a journey
of revenge, dig two graves.**

Everything has yin and yang aspects. Lack of forgiveness results in more pain and suffering, but unconditional love and forgiveness create positivity, including inner joy, inner peace, order, connection, harmony, and opportunities for more love to come into our lives.

When someone or something hurts us, our response can be one of love, forgiveness, peace, connection, and harmony or of the opposite, including anger, irritation, resentment, disconnection, and disharmony. Many people wait for the other person to apologize, or never truly forgive completely. Practicing forgiveness in the moment is the best way to transform negativity and avoid all kinds of further challenges.

~ ~ ~

Let me right away share a one-sentence secret about the root causes of all kinds of life challenges:

The root causes of challenges in health, relationships, finances, business, and the enlightenment journey are soul blockages.

I will explain further.

Ancient wisdom teaches that everyone and everything is made of *shen qi jing.* "Shen" includes soul, heart, and mind (consciousness). "Qi" is energy. "Jing" is matter. A person's health is made of shen qi jing. Every system, every organ, every cell, every DNA, and every RNA in the body is made of shen qi jing. Every relationship is made of shen qi jing. One's finances and businesses are each made of shen qi jing. Mother Earth is made of shen qi jing. Heaven is made of shen qi jing. Countless planets, stars, galaxies, and universes are all made of shen qi jing.

A human being lives on Mother Earth. Heaven is above our heads. Heaven belongs to yang. Mother Earth belongs to yin. We live in the yin-yang world. The number one universal law for Heaven and Mother Earth is the Universal Law of Yin Yang. The core of this universal law is that everyone and everything can be divided into yin and yang. This law is the law of positive and negative.

Therefore, shen qi jing has positive and negative sides. Shen includes soul, heart, and mind. Soul can be positive or negative. Heart and mind can be positive or negative. Qi (energy) and jing (matter) can be positive or negative.

Tao Science, which Dr. and Master Rulin Xiu and I co-created,[1] explains that positive shen qi jing is order, connection, and harmony, while negative shen qi jing is disorder, disconnection, and disharmony.

Why do people get sick?

Why do people have relationship challenges?

Why do people have financial and business challenges?

Why do people have challenges in various aspects of their lives?

In one sentence:

**Challenges in any aspect of life are
due to negative shen qi jing.**

---

[1] See *Tao Science: The Science, Wisdom, and Practice of Creation and Grand Unification*, Cardiff, CA/Richmond Hill, ON: Waterside Press/Heaven's Library Publication Corp., 2017.

How do you transform all life challenges, whether in health, relationships, finances, business, or any aspect of life?

The way to transform all life can also be summarized in one sentence:

To transform all life, including health, relationships, and finances, is to transform negative shen qi jing to positive shen qi jing.

To transform negative shen qi jing to positive shen qi jing, it is important to understand the sacred wisdom of how shen, qi, and jing are related. Shen includes soul, heart, and mind. Soul is information or message. In quantum science and Tao Science:

- Soul is the content or essence of the message.

- Heart (the core of life, which is beyond the physical heart) is the receiver of the message.
- Mind (consciousness) is the processor of the message.
- Qi (energy) is the actioner.
- Jing (matter) is the transformer.

The key sacred wisdom of the relationships among shen, qi, and jing can be summarized in four sentences:

- Soul leads the heart.
- Heart leads the mind.
- Mind leads the qi (energy).
- Qi leads the jing (matter).

Everyone and everything is made of shen qi jing. The sacred wisdom and process of all life can be summarized in one sentence:

The process of all life is: soul leads heart, heart leads mind, mind leads energy, energy leads matter.

Now I am ready to explain the root blockages of all life, including health, relationships, and finances:

The root blockages of all life are soul blockages.

In the spiritual realm, Shi Jia Mo Ni Fo (the Chinese name of Shakyamuni Buddha), the founder of Buddhism, taught, "Yi qie jie you ye suo sheng."

"Yi qie" means *all life, including everyone and everything*. "Jie" means *all*. "You" means *due to*. "Ye" means *the records of all life in actions, behaviors, speech, and thoughts*. "Suo sheng" means *to create*. "Yi qie jie you ye suo sheng" means *all life—everyone and everything—is created by all of one's past actions, behaviors, speech, and thoughts in all past lifetimes and the current lifetime.*

(I deeply believe in reincarnation. You may not. I totally respect your and everyone's belief system. You do not need to agree with me to benefit from the simple practices of forgiveness in this book. In my understanding, all spiritual belief systems teach that when one commits a transgression, one needs to seek and receive forgiveness for it. Thank you for allowing me to share my understanding of our common ground. Thank you for allowing me to serve you through this book.)

All life records, including all previous lifetimes and the current lifetime, can be divided into positive and negative. These records are soul issues. They are carried by the soul. It is important to realize and understand this sacred wisdom.

Positive records of a person, or a company, or a country, or any soul are created when that person, company, country, or soul has served humanity, animals, the environment, and more *positively*, with love, care, compassion, forgiveness, order, connection, and harmony in any lifetime.

Negative records of a person, or a company, or a country, or any soul are created when that person, company, country, or soul has served humanity, animals, the environment, and more *negatively*, by harming or taking advantage of others, cheating, stealing, and creating disorder, disconnection, or disharmony in any lifetime.

These records are universal. All of the actions, behaviors, speech, and thoughts of everyone and everything are recorded, whether positive or negative. These records are controlled by the universe and the Source (Tao). The universe and the Source reward a person who carries positive records through good health, harmonious relationships, flourishing finances and business, and order, connection, and success in any aspect of life.

The universe and the Source teach lessons to a person with negative records through challenges in health, relationships, finances, and business, and disorder, disconnection, and disharmony in any aspect of life.

The deep wisdom to understand is that:

The positive or negative records carried by our soul are the root causes of success and failure in every aspect of our life.

Quantum science teaches about information or message. The spiritual realm teaches about the soul. Tao Science shares with humanity and the scientific community that information or message *is* soul. Soul *is* information or message. Soul issues, which are information or message issues, are the most important issues for life.

Now I can share the greatest value and most powerful significance of this book, *Greatest Forgiveness*.

Greatest forgiveness is the key to addressing the root causes of our challenges: the negative records carried by our soul from all lifetimes.

Millions of people on the spiritual journey believe in Jesus. Remember that Jesus often said, "You are forgiven." All kinds of miracles happened after Jesus offered this forgiveness. It shows us how powerful forgiveness is.

Jesus created miraculous healing because he offered unconditional forgiveness, which is greatest forgiveness. To heal and transform life challenges, it is vital to receive forgiveness. There are two ways to receive forgiveness. One is to receive universal, Divine, or Source forgiveness. The other is to do forgiveness practice.

This book shares with every reader and humanity how to do forgiveness practice in order to transform the root causes of challenges in all life, including health, relationships, and finances. This book further gives you a

Tao Calligraphy (figure 1) that carries shen qi jing of Tao Source. The purest and highest frequencies and vibrations of Tao Source shen qi jing can transform your negative shen qi jing to positive shen qi jing with Source love, Source forgiveness, Source compassion, Source light, and more. This is the priceless value of this book.

The practices are the essential keys to healing and transformation. They yield the benefits proven through clinical research of forgiveness, Chinese calligraphy, and meditation.

I am honored to be a servant to share the sacred wisdom and practical techniques of unconditional and greatest forgiveness.

Forgiveness. Forgiveness. Forgiveness.

Unconditional forgiveness. Unconditional forgiveness. Unconditional forgiveness.

Greatest forgiveness. Greatest forgiveness. Greatest forgiveness.

Heal. Heal. Heal.

Transform. Transform. Transform.
Enlighten. Enlighten. Enlighten.

I love my heart and soul
I love all humanity
Join hearts and souls together
Love, peace, and harmony
Love, peace, and harmony

What Is Greatest Forgiveness?

THINK ABOUT A family. A couple may have challenges. They may be upset with each other and argue. Some may even separate. If forgiveness could be applied within the family, especially unconditional forgiveness, which is the greatest forgiveness, the challenges between the couple could be dissolved.

Think about a workplace. Employees and their managers could have challenges. They may dislike each other. They could have jealousy, competition, ego, and much more. If forgiveness, especially unconditional forgiveness, were applied within the organization, the challenges could be resolved.

Think about different countries and different religions in history. If forgiveness, especially unconditional forgiveness, had been applied, many wars could have been avoided.

As I have explained in the introduction and in many of my other books, when a person is sick, the root cause is soul blockages. The sickness is a lesson taught by the universe and the Source. Therefore, if a person can truly apply forgiveness and be forgiven, the sickness could be healed beyond comprehension.

All kinds of religions and spiritual belief systems have taught the benefits of forgiveness. It is a core teaching and practice that has been a part of human beings' lives and consciousness for thousands of years.

Forgiveness can be divided into two aspects: receiving forgiveness for yourself and offering forgiveness to others. If anyone has harmed, cheated, or taken advantage of you, can you forgive them? If you have made mistakes of hurting or harming others, can you deeply and sincerely apologize and humbly ask for forgiveness? Can you forgive yourself?

There is an even deeper wisdom. If someone harmed you in many lifetimes, across centuries and millennia, can you forgive them? If you harmed others in many lifetimes, can you ask for forgiveness from them?

If you can truly receive and offer the greatest forgiveness, the benefits for you and for others could be beyond your comprehension and imagination. This book will show you how to achieve the blessings of the greatest forgiveness.

What is the greatest forgiveness? It is unconditional forgiveness. Unconditional forgiveness is to forgive completely, without any conditions or expectations. It is to let go totally of any upset, anger, vengefulness, victimization, sense of injustice, anxiety, fear, and more. It can be very hard for people to offer unconditional forgiveness.

I will share two stories. In ancient China, a young unmarried woman became pregnant. Her parents were beyond angry and felt great shame. They asked their daughter who the father was. The daughter said that it was a monk from a nearby temple. This monk was a renowned and revered spiritual father in the local region, which covered thousands of square miles.

The parents went to the temple and yelled at the monk. Although the monk was totally surprised, he remained completely calm. He smiled gently and said, "This is real?" and nothing else.

When the baby was born, the parents gave him to the monk. The monk accepted the baby. When the villagers and more and more people heard what happened, many became very upset with the monk. Some even yelled profanities at the monk and spat on his face.

The monk completely tolerated the insults and said nothing.

Like many monks in that time, this monk had taken a vow of poverty and would beg for food. Whenever he did so, some people would continue to insult the monk very strongly. Despite all the verbal and sometimes physical abuse, the monk kept silent and continued to raise the baby lovingly.

The baby's mother saw everything that happened to the monk. Her heart was so moved by the monk's love, forgiveness, calmness, and forbearance that she was racked with guilt. No longer able to tolerate it, she admitted to her parents that the baby's father was not the monk but rather the fishmonger in the market. The parents deeply regretted what they had done to the monk. They went to the temple to apologize. The monk smiled gently and said, "I forgive you."

This is a story of greatest unconditional forgiveness.

The next story also took place in ancient Asia. A king ordered the execution of a spiritual father by slicing his muscles from head to feet. As he lay bleeding and dying, excruciatingly slowly and painfully, the spiritual father said, "When I meet you again in my next life, I will offer you unconditional forgiveness for killing me now."

In their next lifetimes, this spiritual father did in fact meet the king from their last lifetimes. The spiritual father offered unconditional forgiveness to the king for torturing and killing him in their past lifetimes. This story of unconditional forgiveness is well known in spiritual teaching.

The "stars" of these two stories are great examples of unconditional forgiveness. The first was wrongly accused of and abused for something that was socially disgraceful. He forgave his accusers and abusers unconditionally. The second was killed cruelly. He unconditionally forgave in their next lifetimes the one who ordered his execution. The most renowned example of unconditional forgiveness is Jesus forgiving his executioners as he was crucified.

Some people may not be able to comprehend that this kind of greatest forgiveness is possible. In our current world, when unpleasant things happen, they can lead to lawsuits, revenge, fighting, war, and more. It is very hard to offer unconditional forgiveness to those who have seriously harmed us.

The deepest wisdom is that when we suffer from sickness, relationship challenges, financial and business challenges, and other challenges in life, it is in many cases because we have made mistakes to others in previous lifetimes or in this lifetime. The negative records we or our ancestors have created are the root causes of our challenges. Therefore, a key to resolving our challenges is to ask sincerely for forgiveness from the universe and the Source and from the people that we or our ancestors have harmed in previous lifetimes and in this lifetime.

In other cases, when you are sick or have relationship, financial, or other challenges, you did not necessarily make mistakes in previous lifetimes or the current lifetime.

You may know some of the mistakes you or your ancestors have made. You may not know all of these mistakes, especially from previous lifetimes. It does not matter. Regardless, forgive unconditionally. This is still the key to transform your challenges.

Practicing unconditional forgiveness has two sides.

The first is to ask for forgiveness of our ancestors and ourselves from the universe and the Source, and from those we have harmed.

The second side of forgiveness is to forgive unconditionally those who have harmed you and your ancestors. Forgive completely. Forgive unconditionally. This is another key to transform all life.

The true wisdom of unconditional forgiveness, which is greatest forgiveness, can be summarized as follows:

I forgive you unconditionally.
You forgive me unconditionally.
Bring love, peace, and harmony.

If you truly realize and believe this sacred wisdom, then put forgiveness practice into action. You could receive transformation beyond comprehension for your health, relationships, finances, and business. The stories I share throughout the remaining chapters illustrate this well.

In chapter three, I will share with you the practical techniques and reveal a powerful tool to do forgiveness practice in order to transform every aspect of your life. But first, let us understand better and appreciate more the great transformative power of greatest, unconditional forgiveness.

The Power and Significance of Greatest Forgiveness

FORGIVENESS IS THE key to transform negative shen qi jing.

Unconditional forgiveness, which is greatest forgiveness, can transform negative soul records beyond comprehension. It is the number one way to self-clear and self-transform all kinds of negative shen qi jing, which can block us in every aspect of life.

Negative soul records are the root cause for all challenges in health, relationships, finances, business, and every aspect of life. Therefore, to transform all your life challenges is to remove the root cause, which can be done through unconditional forgiveness.

To transform all your life challenges includes:

- boosting energy, stamina, vitality, and immunity
- healing the physical, emotional, mental, and spiritual bodies
- transforming all kinds of relationships
- transforming finances and business
- opening spiritual communication channels
- increasing intelligence of the soul, heart, mind, and body
- bringing success to every aspect of physical life

- enlightening soul, heart, mind, and body

Sincere forgiveness practice offered unconditionally can transform all life because it can transform the root causes of all challenges. Therefore, forgiveness is the key to transform all life.

The result of sincerely offering unconditional forgiveness is the one-sentence secret about forgiveness that I have shared for many years:

**Forgiveness brings inner
joy and inner peace.**

I would like to share a heartfelt testimony of this one-sentence secret:

Twenty-three years ago, in 1996, I held deep resentment toward someone who I felt had betrayed me. I realized that I needed to move on, and in order to do so, I had to forgive.

One evening, no longer able to carry the pain of resentment in my heart, I asked God for help. I got an immediate and crystal-clear response: Just let it go. *I understood this to mean that it was up to me to hold on or let go. In my heart, in my mind, and from my mouth, I pronounced, "I am ready to let it go." In that moment, the greatest burden was lifted from my being. I was free. It was a very powerful experience of forgiveness.*

I immediately began to see how this single act of forgiveness impacted my life. My relationship with this person improved dramatically, and I saw other areas of my life where forgiveness was needed. When I began studying with Master Sha in 2005, I learned more about the power and significance of forgiveness on the spiritual journey and in one's physical life and began doing forgiveness practice regularly. Since then I have experienced many times how offering and receiving forgiveness can transform not only my life but others' too.

Every single time I do forgiveness practice, even for a few minutes, I feel a shift. Many times, I notice that not only do I feel lighter, the physical space around me also feels more spacious, as though obstacles around me have been removed.

In fact, I know deeply in my heart that obstacles have been removed. Negativity has transformed to positivity. Since forgiveness has become an integral part of my daily life, I know what true freedom, joy, and peace are.

Li An Di
New York

~ ~ ~

The significance of offering and receiving forgiveness cannot be overstated. As I shared earlier, the root cause of blockages in health, emotions, relationships, finances, business, and more is our negative records from all lifetimes. In order to transform the blockages in any aspect of life, we have to transform the negative records. Forgiveness practice is the most powerful way to do this.

In *Dao De Jing*, Lao Zi taught that to be humble is to be like water. Water humbly flows to the lowest places, serving unconditionally, asking for nothing. Practice forgiveness with an open heart, great sincerity, and humility. Practice forgiveness in the moment so that forgiveness becomes a way of life. It can take time to develop the habit of forgiveness, but the benefits for your physical life and spiritual journey, including true inner joy and peace, can be the greatest rewards.[2]

~ ~ ~

Unconditional greatest forgiveness must come from all levels of the soul, heart, mind, and body. The key is for it to come from the heart and soul levels. *Sincerity and honesty move people, Heaven, and souls.*

Forgiveness is not a one-time practice. Forgiveness has layers and is a gradual process that occurs over time for most people.

Forgiveness opens the heart and soul.

Forgiveness is one of the golden keys to unlock the door to advancing in every aspect of life.

_____

[2] For more on transforming relationships through forgiveness, see chapter ten in my book *The Power of Soul: The Way to Heal, Rejuvenate, and Enlighten All Life*, New York/Toronto: Atria Books/Heaven's Library Publication Corp., 2009.

The more forgiveness practice you do, the more flourishing you could achieve in every aspect of life.

Forgiveness is the key to bring love, peace, and harmony.

Apply Greatest Forgiveness with the Tao Calligraphy *Da Kuan Shu* to Transform All Life

I AM DELIGHTED to share practical techniques to transform all life by applying greatest forgiveness unconditionally.

Apply the following practical Five Power Techniques to transform all of your life with unconditional greatest forgiveness. The Five Power Techniques are:

1. **Body Power.** Body Power is special body, hand, and finger positions for healing, rejuvenation, and transformation. In one sentence:

> **Where you put your hands is where you receive benefits.**

2. **Soul Power.** Soul Power is to *say hello*. To *say hello* is to invoke outer souls such as Tao Source, the Divine, spiritual fathers and mothers, Heaven, Mother Earth, and countless planets, stars, galaxies, and universes. It is also to invoke inner souls of one's own soul, heart, mind, and body. In one sentence:

> **Whomever you invoke is who offers you benefits.**

3. **Mind Power.** Mind Power is creative visualization. In one sentence:

What you visualize is what blesses you.

4. **Sound Power.** Sound Power is to repeatedly chant or sing special mantras or vibratory sounds. In one sentence:

What you chant is what you become.

5. **Tracing Power.** Tracing Power is to connect with and trace Tao Calligraphy. Tao Calligraphy is calligraphy of the Source. It carries Source shen qi jing for healing, rejuvenation, and transformation of all life. In this book, I give you the Tao Calligraphy *Da Kuan Shu* (figure 1, following page 56). "Da" means *greatest*. "Kuan shu" means *forgiveness*. So "Da Kuan Shu" (pronounced *dah kwahn shoo*) means *greatest forgiveness*.

~ ~ ~

*For the last three decades, scientists have
conducted research on medical therapy
interventions of Chinese calligraphy
handwriting. Clinical research has found
Chinese calligraphy handwriting has positive
effects on behavioral and psychosomatic
disorders: depressive symptoms in cancer
patients, psychiatric and cognitive disorders
in elderly people, stress levels, hyperarousal
symptoms after earthquake, changes in theta
waves, and diseases such as hypertension
and attention deficit hyperactivity disorder.*

~ ~ ~

Tao Calligraphy is Oneness writing to transform all life. Tao Calligraphies:

- carry a Tao Source Field, which
  consists of the pure, positive shen qi

jing (soul, heart, mind, energy, and matter) of Tao Source;

- carry Tao Source frequency, vibration, love, forgiveness, compassion, light, and more;
- connect with all kinds of spiritual fathers and mothers in Heaven;
- can transform negative shen qi jing fields to positive shen qi jing fields;
- carry high-level Tao blessing power for every aspect of life, including health, relationships, finances, business, intelligence, the spiritual journey, and more.

Because Tao Calligraphies bring great power to heal, bless, and transform all life, I have included at least one Tao Calligraphy in all my books since 2013. You can learn more about Tao Calligraphy in my recent book

Tao Chang Tao Calligraphy: The Source Field to Transform All Life.[3] In one sentence:

What you trace is what you become.

Apply these Five Power Techniques to transform your physical, emotional, mental, and spiritual health, your relationships, your finances and business, and every aspect of your life.

Transform Health

Physical Body

For any sickness, disease, pain, inflammation, tumor, cancer, or other physical health condition, apply the Five Power Techniques as follows:

[3] Cardiff, CA/Richmond Hill, ON: Waterside Press/Heaven's Library Publication Corp., 2019.

Body Power. Place one palm on your lower abdomen below your navel. Your lower abdomen is a foundational area for your soul, heart, mind, energy, and matter. Place your other palm over the organ, part of the body, or area for which you want healing. Remember, *where you put your hands is where you receive benefits.*

Soul Power. *Say hello* to outer souls and inner souls (*whomever you invoke is who offers you benefits*):

> *Dear Source and Divine,*
> *Dear all spiritual fathers and mothers*
>   *in all realms,*
> *Dear Heaven and Mother Earth,*
> *Dear countless planets, stars, galaxies,*
>   *and universes,*
> *Dear all the souls my ancestors or I*
>   *have harmed in this lifetime and all*
>   *lifetimes,*

Dear shen qi jing of _____ (name the system, organ, part of the body, or physical health condition, such as hypertension, diabetes, a tumor, cancer, or pain, for which you want healing),

I love you all.

Please forgive my ancestors and me for the mistakes we have made in this lifetime and all lifetimes.

We unconditionally forgive anyone who harmed my ancestors or me in all lifetimes.

Please give me healing, blessing, rejuvenation, and transformation for _____ (repeat your request for the physical body).

I am extremely grateful.

Thank you.

Mind Power. Visualize golden light shining in the area of your request.

Remember, *what you visualize is what blesses you*. Light heals, blesses, rejuvenates; and transforms. Ancient wisdom teaches *jin guang zhao ti, bai bing xiao chu*, which means *golden light shines in the body, all sicknesses are removed*.

Sound Power. Chant or sing this three-line forgiveness mantra repeatedly:

> *I forgive you unconditionally.*
> *You forgive me unconditionally.*
> *Bring love, peace, and harmony.*

Remember, *what you chant is what you become*. You are becoming unconditional greatest forgiveness. Those you have harmed are becoming unconditional greatest forgiveness. Those who have harmed you are becoming unconditional greatest forgiveness. Love, peace, and harmony are coming to you, to those you have harmed, and to those who have harmed you.

Tracing Power. Trace the Tao Calligraphy *Da Kuan Shu* (Greatest Forgiveness) along its oneness path (figure 2, following page 56) with the five fingertips of one hand together. See figure 3 on the next page.

Chant and trace for at least ten minutes. *What you trace is what you become.* The longer you chant and trace, the better the results you could receive. For chronic and serious (for example, life-threatening) conditions, chant and trace for a total of two hours per day. You can split the time into several practice sessions, but your total practice time should be at least two hours each day.

Close. End your healing, blessing, rejuvenation, and transformation practice session by saying:

> *Hao. Hao. Hao.* (Mandarin Chinese for *good, perfect, healthy,* pronounced *how*)

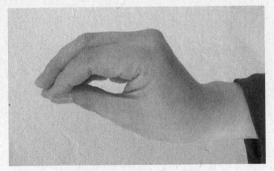

Figure 3. Five Fingers Hand
Position for Tracing Power

Thank you. Thank you. Thank you. (to
   all the souls who supported your
   practice)
Gong song. Gong song. Gong song.
   (Mandarin Chinese for *respectfully
   return to your abode* to the outer souls
   you invoked, pronounced *gōng sōng*
   with long o's as in *oh*)

~ ~ ~

*According to a 2016 study, people are more
sensitive to pain when they feel a sense
of injustice. Sincere forgiveness helps one
let go of any resentment, victimization,
or other responses with negative shen qi
jing. Reduced physical pain can follow.*

~ ~ ~

I would like to share how one student has
benefited frequently from forgiveness practice, physically and emotionally:

*It took me quite some time to under-
stand the value and power of forgiveness
practice, and I am sure my understanding can still deepen and increase.*

*Whenever I have any kind of pain, I
do a forgiveness practice. By doing so and
empowering the practice with my heart*

and soul, I have comforted various pains in my body on a regular basis, including head, neck, and stomach aches.

It is still surprising to me that I experience relief from pain by doing this. And it is the same when I am stuck in anger and ill will for another person, or simply a deep disappointment in life itself. In these situations as well, I have received relief from these feelings.

Every time I experience this, the deeper my understanding of the significance of forgiveness becomes. I am very grateful.

Femke S.
Germany

~ ~ ~

All the practices in this chapter are *active actions* for healing and transformation. Relax through the Sound Power (chanting of the three-line forgiveness mantra) and Tracing Power (following the oneness path of the Tao Calligraphy *Da Kuan Shu*). You could feel your challenges melting away.

Let us now practice forgiveness with Tao Calligraphy tracing to balance and transform unbalanced emotions.

Emotional Body

Challenges in the emotional body include anger, depression, anxiety, worry, sadness, grief, fear, and more.

You probably have experienced emotional imbalances leading to a loss of energy, lowering of immunity, or a physical ailment. For five thousand years, ancient Chinese philosophy and traditional Chinese medicine have understood a strong connection between the emotional body and the physical body. They link specific emotions with specific organs through the Five Elements theory.

Five Elements theory and practice have guided millions of people in history to heal sickness and to rejuvenate soul, heart, mind, and body. The Five Elements of nature (Wood, Fire, Earth, Metal, and Water) summarize and categorize the internal organs, sensory organs, bodily tissues, emotional body, and more. See figure 4 on the next page for the essence of this wisdom.

We will apply this Five Elements wisdom in the following practices to heal and transform our negative shen qi jing associated with various imbalances in the emotional body.

Heal and Transform Anger

Anger can be linked to hostility and can arise from an inability to forgive. A ten-year study completed in 2018 with a national sample of American adults found that greater hostility is associated with the development of more cognitive impairment,

Element	Yin Organ	Yang Organ	Body Tissue	Sense	Unbalanced Emotion	Balanced Emotion	Finger
Wood	Liver	Gallbladder	Tendons Nails	Eyes Sight	Anger	Patience	Index
Fire	Heart	Small Intestine	Blood Vessels	Tongue Taste	Depression Anxiety Excitability	Joy	Middle
Earth	Spleen	Stomach	Muscles	Mouth Lips Speech	Worry	Love Compassion	Thumb
Metal	Lungs	Large Intestine	Skin	Nose Smell	Grief Sadness	Courage	Ring
Water	Kidneys	Urinary Bladder	Bones Joints	Ears Hearing	Fear	Calmness	Little

Figure 4. Five Elements

*and that being more forgiving, especially
more self-forgiving, mitigates these effects.*

~ ~ ~

Body Power. Place one palm on your lower abdomen below your navel. Your lower abdomen is a foundational area for your soul, heart, mind, energy, and matter. Place your other palm over your liver. The liver connects with anger within the Wood element. *Where you put your hands is where you receive benefits.*

Soul Power. *Say hello* to outer souls and inner souls (*whomever you invoke is who offers you benefits*):

> *Dear Source and Divine,*
> *Dear all spiritual fathers and mothers*
>   *in all realms,*
> *Dear Heaven and Mother Earth,*

Dear countless planets, stars, galaxies, and universes,
Dear all the souls my ancestors or I have harmed in any way related to anger in this lifetime and all lifetimes,
Dear shen qi jing of my liver,
I love you all.
Please forgive my ancestors and me for the mistakes we have made in this lifetime and all lifetimes related to anger, where we have been angry at others or made others angry.
We unconditionally forgive anyone who caused anger in my ancestors or me or who hurt us with anger in all lifetimes.
Please heal and transform my anger.
I am extremely grateful.
Thank you.

Mind Power. Visualize your liver shining golden light. *What you visualize is what blesses you.*

Sound Power. Chant or sing repeatedly (*what you chant is what you become*):

> *I forgive you unconditionally.*
> *You forgive me unconditionally.*
> *Bring love, peace, and harmony.*

Tracing Power. Trace the Tao Calligraphy *Da Kuan Shu* (Greatest Forgiveness) along its oneness path (figure 2) using the Five Fingers Hand Position (figure 3). *What you trace is what you become.* The Five Fingers Hand Position has great power to heal, bless, rejuvenate, and transform because each finger represents one of the Five Elements. Therefore, you are connecting the shen qi jing of all five of your elements with the shen qi jing of Tao Source.

Chant and trace for at least ten minutes. The longer you chant and trace, the better the results you could receive. If you have chronic or serious anger issues, chant and trace for a total of two hours per day. You can split the time into several practice sessions, but your total practice time should be at least two hours.

Close. End your healing and transformational practice session by saying:

> Hao. Hao. Hao.
> Thank you. Thank you. Thank you.
> Gong song. Gong song. Gong song.

~ ~ ~

The healing practices I lead you to do carry many of the proven benefits of meditation. The calm, relaxed meditative state that you could reach when tracing Tao Calligraphy helps to explain its benefits. When you meditate, your brain cells develop new connections. The brain's physical structure actually changes, strengthening the part of your brain that regulates emotions, especially counteracting negative feelings of fear, anxiety, and depression. The longer you practice, the more enduring the changes.

Heal and Transform Depression and Anxiety

Body Power. Place one palm on your lower abdomen below your navel. Place your other palm over your heart. The heart connects with depression and anxiety within the Fire element. You may have experienced, or heard someone speak of, a "heavy" or "fluttering" heart.

Soul Power. *Say hello* to outer souls and inner souls:

> *Dear Source and Divine,*
> *Dear all spiritual fathers and mothers*
>   *in all realms,*

Dear Heaven and Mother Earth,

Dear countless planets, stars, galaxies, and universes,

Dear all the souls my ancestors or I have harmed in any way related to depression and anxiety in this lifetime and all lifetimes,

Dear shen qi jing of my heart,

I love you all.

Please forgive my ancestors and me for the mistakes we have made in this lifetime and all lifetimes causing others to be depressed or anxious, or where we have hurt others through our depression or anxiety.

We unconditionally forgive anyone who caused depression or anxiety in my ancestors or me in all lifetimes.

Please heal and transform my depression and anxiety.

I am extremely grateful.

Thank you.

Mind Power. Visualize your heart shining golden light.

Sound Power. Chant or sing repeatedly:

> *I forgive you unconditionally.*
> *You forgive me unconditionally.*
> *Bring love, peace, and harmony.*

Tracing Power. Trace the Tao Calligraphy *Da Kuan Shu* (Greatest Forgiveness) along its oneness path (figure 2) using the Five Fingers Hand Position (figure 3).

Chant and trace for at least ten minutes. The longer you chant and trace, the better the results you could receive. If you have chronic or serious depression or anxiety, chant and trace for a total of two hours per day. You can split the time into several practice sessions, but your total practice time should be at least two hours.

Close. End your healing and transformational practice session by saying:

> *Hao. Hao. Hao.*
> *Thank you. Thank you. Thank you.*
> *Gong song. Gong song. Gong song.*

Heal and Transform Worry

Body Power. Place one palm on your lower abdomen below your navel. Place your other palm over your spleen. The spleen connects with worry within the Earth element.

Soul Power. *Say hello* to outer souls and inner souls:

> *Dear Source and Divine,*
> *Dear all spiritual fathers and mothers*
>   *in all realms,*
> *Dear Heaven and Mother Earth,*
> *Dear countless planets, stars, galaxies,*
>   *and universes,*

Dear all the souls my ancestors or I have
harmed in any way related to worry
in this lifetime and all lifetimes,
Dear shen qi jing of my spleen,
I love you all.
Please forgive my ancestors and me
for the mistakes we have made in
this lifetime and all lifetimes caus-
ing others to be worried or where we
have hurt others through our worry.
We unconditionally forgive anyone who
caused worry in my ancestors or me
in all lifetimes.
Please heal and transform my worry.
I am extremely grateful.
Thank you.

Mind Power. Visualize your spleen shining golden light.

Sound Power. Chant or sing repeatedly:

I forgive you unconditionally.
You forgive me unconditionally.
Bring love, peace, and harmony.

Tracing Power. Trace the Tao Calligraphy *Da Kuan Shu* (Greatest Forgiveness) along its oneness path (figure 2) using the Five Fingers Hand Position (figure 3).

Chant and trace for at least ten minutes. The longer you chant and trace, the better the results you could receive. If you are a chronic or serious worrier, chant and trace for a total of two hours per day. You can split the time into several practice sessions, but your total practice time should be at least two hours.

Close. End your healing and transformational practice session by saying:

Hao. Hao. Hao.
Thank you. Thank you. Thank you.
Gong song. Gong song. Gong song.

Heal and Transform Sadness and Grief

Body Power. Place one palm on your lower abdomen below your navel. Place your other palm over a lung. (If you wish, you may move this palm from one lung to the other during the practice.) The lungs connect with sadness and grief within the Metal element.

Soul Power. *Say hello* to outer souls and inner souls:

> *Dear Source and Divine,*
> *Dear all spiritual fathers and mothers*
>   *in all realms,*
> *Dear Heaven and Mother Earth,*
> *Dear countless planets, stars, galaxies,*
>   *and universes,*
> *Dear all the souls my ancestors or I have*
>   *harmed in any way related to sad-*
>   *ness and grief in this lifetime and all*
>   *lifetimes,*
> *Dear shen qi jing of my lungs,*

I love you all.

Please forgive my ancestors and me for the mistakes we have made in this lifetime and all lifetimes causing others to be sad or grieving, or where we have hurt others through our sadness or grief.

We unconditionally forgive anyone who caused sadness or grief in my ancestors or me in all lifetimes.

Please heal and transform my sadness and grief.

I am extremely grateful.

Thank you.

Mind Power. Visualize your lungs shining golden light.

Sound Power. Chant or sing repeatedly:

I forgive you unconditionally.
You forgive me unconditionally.

Bring love, peace, and harmony.

Tracing Power. Trace the Tao Calligraphy *Da Kuan Shu* (Greatest Forgiveness) along its oneness path (figure 2) using the Five Fingers Hand Position (figure 3).

Chant and trace for at least ten minutes. The longer you chant and trace, the better the results you could receive. If you have chronic or deep sadness or grief, chant and trace for a total of two hours per day. You can split the time into several practice sessions, but your total practice time should be at least two hours.

Close. End your healing and transformational practice session by saying:

Hao. Hao. Hao.
Thank you. Thank you. Thank you.
Gong song. Gong song. Gong song.

~ ~ ~

*A 2016 psychotherapeutic meta-analysis
concluded that using theoretically grounded
forgiveness interventions is a sound
choice for helping clients to deal with
past offenses and helping them achieve
resolution in the form of forgiveness.*

~ ~ ~

Heal and Transform Fear

Body Power. Place one palm on your lower abdomen below your navel. Place your other palm over a kidney. (If you wish, you may alternate between kidneys during the practice.) The kidneys connect with fear within the Water element.

Soul Power. *Say hello* to outer souls and inner souls:

Dear Source and Divine,

Dear all spiritual fathers and mothers in all realms,

Dear Heaven and Mother Earth,

Dear countless planets, stars, galaxies, and universes,

Dear all the souls my ancestors or I have harmed in any way related to fear in this lifetime and all lifetimes,

Dear shen qi jing of my kidneys,

I love you all.

Please forgive my ancestors and me for the mistakes we have made in this lifetime and all lifetimes causing others to be fearful or frightened, or where we have hurt others through our fear.

We unconditionally forgive anyone who caused fear in my ancestors or me in all lifetimes.

Please heal and transform my fear.

I am extremely grateful.

Thank you.

Mind Power. Visualize your kidneys shining golden light.

Sound Power. Chant or sing repeatedly:

> *I forgive you unconditionally.*
> *You forgive me unconditionally.*
> *Bring love, peace, and harmony.*

Tracing Power. Trace the Tao Calligraphy *Da Kuan Shu* (Greatest Forgiveness) along its oneness path (figure 2) using the Five Fingers Hand Position (figure 3).

Chant and trace for at least ten minutes. The longer you chant and trace, the better the results you could receive. If you have chronic or serious fears, chant and trace for a total of two hours per day. You can split the time into several practice sessions, but your total practice time should be at least two hours.

Close. End your healing and transformational practice session by saying:

> *Hao. Hao. Hao.*
> *Thank you. Thank you. Thank you.*
> *Gong song. Gong song. Gong song.*

~ ~ ~

*Using brain imaging technology, scientists have
found that the act of meditating engages the
frontal lobe connections that directly influence the
brain's limbic system, which controls emotions.
The first study to show these alterations was
published in the journal NeuroReport in
2005. Researchers used MRI scans to compare
the brains of longtime meditators, who had
practiced an average of nine years, to those of
people who didn't engage in meditation. The
findings showed that people who meditated had
a thicker cerebral cortex, the area of the brain*

*responsible for information processing, than those
who didn't. Current research has shown benefits
can begin to occur in as little as eight weeks.*

~ ~ ~

Mental Body

I am delighted to share ancient sacred wisdom and practice. The secret wisdom is that
the heart houses the mind and the soul.
Therefore, for any mental challenges and conditions, the secret practice is to use the heart
to heal.

Body Power. Place one palm on your lower
abdomen below your navel. Your lower
abdomen is a foundational area for your soul,
heart, mind, energy, and matter. Place your
other palm over your heart.

Soul Power. *Say hello* to outer souls and inner
souls:

Dear Source and Divine,
Dear all spiritual fathers and mothers
in all realms,
Dear Heaven and Mother Earth,
Dear countless planets, stars, galaxies,
and universes,
Dear all the souls my ancestors or I have
harmed in any way related to mental
challenges and conditions in this life-
time and all lifetimes,
Dear shen qi jing of my heart and mind,
I love you all.
Please forgive my ancestors and me for
the mistakes we have made in this
lifetime and all lifetimes causing
mental challenges and conditions in
others and for the times we have hurt
others through our mental challenges.
We unconditionally forgive anyone who
caused mental challenges in my
ancestors or me in all lifetimes.

Please heal my _____
　　(name your mental condition or
　　make a request for your mind,
　　e.g., remove negative mind-sets,
　　attitudes, or beliefs, remove ego or
　　attachments, remove judgment,
　　remove self-doubt, etc.).
I am extremely grateful.
Thank you.

Mind Power. Visualize your heart and mind shining golden light.

Sound Power. Chant or sing repeatedly:

I forgive you unconditionally.
You forgive me unconditionally.
Bring love, peace, and harmony.

Tracing Power. Trace the Tao Calligraphy *Da Kuan Shu* (Greatest Forgiveness) along its oneness path (figure 2) using the Five Fingers Hand Position (figure 3).

Chant and trace for at least ten minutes. The longer you chant and trace, the better the results you could receive. If you have chronic or serious mental blockages or conditions, chant and trace for a total of two hours per day. You can split the time into several practice sessions, but your total practice time should be at least two hours.

Close. End your healing and transformational practice session by saying:

Hao. Hao. Hao.
Thank you. Thank you. Thank you.
Gong song. Gong song. Gong song.

Spiritual Body

I have shared the sacred wisdom and practice to heal the mental body: the heart houses the mind and the soul. Therefore, to heal the spiritual body is also to use the heart to heal.

Body Power. Place one palm on your lower abdomen below your navel. Your lower abdomen is a foundational area for your soul, heart, mind, energy, and matter. Place your other palm over your heart.

Soul Power. *Say hello* to outer souls and inner souls:

> *Dear Source and Divine,*
> *Dear all spiritual fathers and mothers*
>   *in all realms,*
> *Dear Heaven and Mother Earth,*
> *Dear countless planets, stars, galaxies,*
>   *and universes,*
> *Dear all the souls my ancestors or I have*
>   *harmed in any way related to the*
>   *spiritual journey in this lifetime and*
>   *all lifetimes,*
> *Dear shen qi jing of my heart,*

Figure 1. Tao Calligraphy Da Kuan Shu

Start

Figure 2. Oneness path of Tao
Calligraphy *Da Kuan Shu*

I love you all.

Please forgive my ancestors and me for the mistakes we have made in this lifetime and all lifetimes causing any challenges in anyone's spiritual journey.

We unconditionally forgive anyone who caused challenges in the spiritual journey for my ancestors or me in all lifetimes.

Please heal my spiritual body and bless my spiritual journey.

I am extremely grateful.

Thank you.

Mind Power. Visualize your heart shining golden light.

Sound Power. Chant or sing repeatedly:

I forgive you unconditionally.
You forgive me unconditionally.

Bring love, peace, and harmony.

Tracing Power. Trace the Tao Calligraphy *Da Kuan Shu* (Greatest Forgiveness) along its oneness path (figure 2) using the Five Fingers Hand Position (figure 3).

Chant and trace for at least ten minutes. The longer you chant and trace, the better the results you could receive.

Close. End your healing and transformational practice session by saying:

Hao. Hao. Hao.
Thank you. Thank you. Thank you.
Gong song. Gong song. Gong song.

Transform Relationships

Relationships are a huge issue for humanity. We have a relationship with everyone and everything in our lives. We have family, friend, and work relationships. Organizations and businesses have relationships. We have relationships with organizations and businesses. Cities and countries have relationships. We have relationships with cities and countries. All these relationships and more can deeply affect our lives.

I am delighted to release wisdom of a sacred and secret area for healing all kinds of relationships. This area is inside the body just in front of the Ming Men acupuncture point. "Ming" means *life*. "Men" means *gate*. Ming Men is the *life gate*. The Ming Men acupuncture point is located on the lower back directly behind the navel. The sacred and secret area connected to the Ming Men point is fist-sized. See figure 5 on page 61. This is the sacred area to heal all relationships.

Body Power. Place one palm over your navel. Place your other palm on your back over the Ming Men acupuncture point, directly behind your navel.

Soul Power. *Say hello to outer souls and inner souls:*

> *Dear Source and Divine,*
> *Dear all spiritual fathers and mothers in all realms,*
> *Dear Heaven and Mother Earth,*
> *Dear countless planets, stars, galaxies, and universes,*
> *Dear all the souls my ancestors or I have harmed in any way related to relationships in this lifetime and all lifetimes,*
> *Dear shen qi jing of my Ming Men point and connected area,*
> *I love you all.*
> *Please forgive my ancestors and me for the mistakes we have made in this lifetime and all lifetimes causing any challenges in anyone's relationships.*

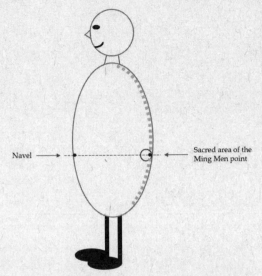

Figure 5. Ming Men point and connected sacred and secret area for relationships

We unconditionally forgive anyone who harmed any relationships of my ancestors or me in all lifetimes.

Please heal my relationships with
_____ (name the relation-
ships for which you are requesting healing).
I am extremely grateful.
Thank you.

Mind Power. Visualize your Ming Men point and connected area shining golden light.

Sound Power. Chant or sing repeatedly:

I forgive you unconditionally.
You forgive me unconditionally.
Bring love, peace, and harmony.

Tracing Power. Trace the Tao Calligraphy *Da Kuan Shu* (Greatest Forgiveness) along its oneness path (figure 2) using the Five Fingers Hand Position (figure 3).

Chant and trace for at least ten minutes. The longer you chant and trace, the better the results you could receive. If you have chronic or serious relationship challenges, chant and trace for a total of two hours per day. You can split the time into several practice sessions, but your total practice time should be at least two hours.

Close. End your healing and transformational practice session by saying:

> *Hao. Hao. Hao.*
> *Thank you. Thank you. Thank you.*
> *Gong song. Gong song. Gong song.*

~ ~ ~

Here is a short, sweet story about the power of forgiveness to transform a relationship blockage—in fifteen minutes:

> *I felt some tension between my wife and*
> *me as she walked out of the room one*

night, so I picked up the Greatest Love book[4] and found a forgiveness practice for relationships. I traced the Tao Source Calligraphy in the book for around fifteen minutes and felt the tension leave.

My wife came back in the room shortly after and she was full of smiles. The tension between us was gone!

Tim Jones
Oregon

~ ~ ~

See chapter four for additional heart-touching experiences of the power of forgiveness to heal and transform relationships.

---

[4] *Greatest Love: Unblock Your Life in 30 Minutes a Day with the Power of Unconditional Love*, Dallas, Texas/Richmond Hill, ON: BenBella Books/Heaven's Library Publication Corp., 2017.

Transform Finances and Business

I am delighted to release another sacred and secret wisdom to transform finances and business. In ancient soul, heart, mind, and body practice, there is a sacred area located in the lower abdomen. It is named Lower Dan Tian and is well known to energy practitioners, including tai chi and qigong practitioners, and martial artists.

The Lower Dan Tian is fist-sized and is centered two or three inches below the navel, slightly closer to the front of the body than to the back. See figure 6.

This area can transform the shen qi jing of finances and business beyond comprehension.

Body Power. Place one palm over your navel. Place your other palm immediately below, to fully cover your Lower Dan Tian.

Soul Power. *Say hello* to outer souls and inner souls:

Dear Source and Divine,
Dear all spiritual fathers and mothers
   in all realms,
Dear Heaven and Mother Earth,
Dear countless planets, stars, galaxies,
   and universes,

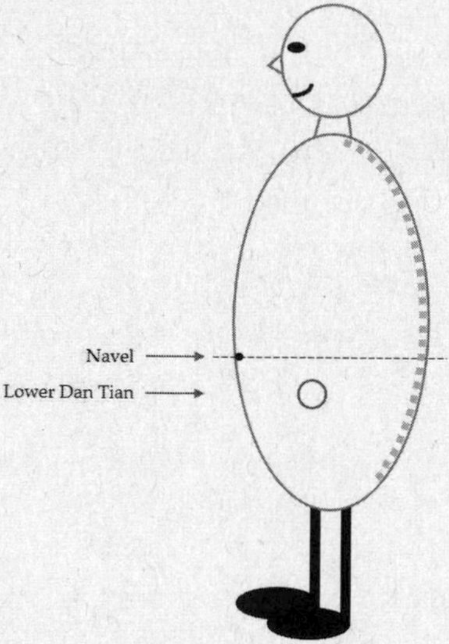

Navel ⟶
Lower Dan Tian ⟶

Figure 6. Lower Dan Tian—sacred and
secret area for finances and business

Dear all the souls my ancestors or I have harmed in any way related to money or business in this lifetime and all lifetimes,

Dear shen qi jing of my Lower Dan Tian,

I love you all.

Please forgive my ancestors and me for the mistakes we have made in this lifetime and all lifetimes causing any challenges in anyone's finances or business.

We unconditionally forgive anyone who harmed the finances or businesses of my ancestors or me in all lifetimes.

Please heal and transform my finances and business.

I am extremely grateful.

Thank you.

Mind Power. Visualize your Lower Dan Tian shining golden light.

Sound Power. Chant or sing repeatedly:

> *I forgive you unconditionally.*
> *You forgive me unconditionally.*
> *Bring love, peace, and harmony.*

Tracing Power. Trace the Tao Calligraphy *Da Kuan Shu* (Greatest Forgiveness) along its oneness path (figure 2) using the Five Fingers Hand Position (figure 3).

Chant and trace for at least ten minutes. The longer you chant and trace, the better the results you could receive.

Close. End your healing and transformational practice session by saying:

> *Hao. Hao. Hao.*
> *Thank you. Thank you. Thank you.*
> *Gong song. Gong song. Gong song.*

~ ~ ~

I would like to share a story of an unexpected financial blessing that came after doing forgiveness practice:

> Forgiveness practice has helped me transform many areas of my life. One powerful experience I had while doing a forgiveness practice was in 2012 when Master Sha asked his students in an advanced program to practice forgiveness for one hour a day for thirty days.
>
> The practice itself is simple and direct. However, when my blockages come up, it can take everything in me to actually do the practice! At that time, I was experiencing a financial challenge and I really needed extra money as soon as possible.
>
> One day I had gone all day avoiding my forgiveness practice and doing

everything else—washing dishes, vacuuming, walking the dog, and more.

I finally exhausted my options, so I surrendered to the practice. I sat down and literally forced myself to do an invocation and began to sing the heart song Love, Peace and Harmony.[5] *I felt irritated at first, but after about twenty to thirty minutes of singing I had a huge release and started to cry. Once this happened, I immediately felt better and continued to sing for the rest of the hour. At exactly the sixty-minute mark, I heard a ding on my phone indicating that I had received a text. I closed the practice and read my text. It was a notice of a payment from a source that was totally unexpected. It was for hundreds of dollars! An immediate financial blessing!*

---

[5] See LovePeaceHarmony.org for more information and a free mp3 download of this song that you can apply in your forgiveness practice.

I am so grateful for the practice of forgiveness, which empowers us to purify our hearts, souls, minds, and bodies. Now I practice at least once a day, as well as in the moment when any challenge or discord arises.

Practice forgiveness. If everyone would practice forgiveness, what a different world we would live in.

Pamela Carmo
Florida

~ ~ ~

Doing forgiveness practice with Tao Calligraphy tracing is one of the most powerful techniques to transform every aspect of your life.

Practice. Practice. Practice.

Forgive. Forgive. Forgive.

Be forgiven. Be forgiven. Be forgiven.

The more forgiveness practice you do, the more flourishing and success you could achieve in every aspect of life.

Forgiveness is the key to bring love, peace, and harmony.

4

Additional Heart-Touching Stories of Forgiveness

IN 1990, NELSON Mandela, recently released after almost thirty years in a South African prison, told a rally, "We especially need to forgive each other, because when you intend to forgive, you heal part of the pain, but when you forgive you heal completely."

Many scientific, psychological, and social research studies have shown the great breadth of benefits that come with forgiveness. These benefits have been demonstrated for health, happiness, stress levels, mental health, relationships, academic performance, social adaptation, spiritual health, and more.

Forgiveness has great benefits not only for the person forgiving and the person being forgiven; it benefits our families, loved ones, relationships, workplaces, ancestors, communities, societies, countries, and Mother Earth. Archbishop Desmond Tutu led South Africa's Truth and Reconciliation Commission as its chairman to encourage forgiveness and reconciliation after the end of apartheid in that country. He believes that forgiveness is the way to "true enduring peace."

In this chapter, I am delighted to share intimately personal stories of the power of forgiveness to heal and transform. Each of the authors of these stories has been deeply moved. Their healing, transformation, and gratitude are so heart-touching.

May these stories inspire you to do sincere forgiveness practice more.

Relationships

Challenging family relationship transformed with forgiveness practice

My only sister had not spoken to me in over ten years and I didn't know why. If I entered a room she was in, she would leave. She did not respond when I sent her emails or cards. The matter finally came to a climax when we were both in our fifties. My sister physically attacked me at our parents' house. When I raised my hands to cover my face as she was hitting me, her dog construed it as an aggressive act toward her, and he bit me. I was enraged and confused, yet I got little to no support from my family when I tried to discuss it with them.

When I first learned of forgiveness practice, I immediately called my sister's soul to do a practice daily. During the first week, resistance was extreme, but by the second week I felt more of a flow. When I visited my parents' house during the third week, she actually talked to me!

I now do forgiveness practice every day, sometimes for hours at a time. My relationships have become much lighter, happier, and forgiving. I deeply appreciate this most beneficial practice.

Janet Jaworski
Syracuse, New York

Blockages are removed and love remains

I had been a very close friend with someone for twenty-five years. We saw *each other or spoke on the phone almost every day. One day we had a disagreement about something very insignificant. She hung up the phone on me and sent me an email asking me not to contact her again. I was devastated and heartbroken, but I respected her wishes and didn't contact her.*

A few years went by and I started studying with Master Sha. I decided to try doing forgiveness practice with her soul. A few weeks later, she sent me an email saying, "I am sure you don't want to ever talk to me again, but I want you to know how much I love you, miss you, and think about you all the time." I responded saying that I loved her too and forgave her unconditionally. We spoke on the phone and have been friends again for the past year. Through forgiveness, the blockage was removed and the love remained. I am so grateful. Forgiveness is so beautiful!

L. S.
New Hampshire

No more strained relationships!

I had read that one must forgive, forget, and let go. I used to do forgiveness but it was just verbal and I could not see any benefit.

My husband's brother and his family were not on speaking terms with us and the relationship between his sisters was also strained.

After becoming a soul healing practitioner, I understood the importance of forgiveness and did daily forgiveness practice and sang the heart song Love,

Peace and Harmony.[6] *Forgiveness practice not only brought inner joy and inner peace but also brought light to our strained relationships and transformed them into love. Now the relationships are good and I can see the love and happiness in all the family members.*

My relationships, finances, health, and many other issues have transformed with forgiveness practice. Whenever I face any challenge, I do a forgiveness practice and I can see the challenge transforming. Words of gratitude for the powerful forgiveness practices are very small compared to the blessings received.

Rashmi M.
India

---

[6] See LovePeaceHarmony.org for more information and a free mp3 download of this song that you can apply in your forgiveness practice.

Reconciliation after twenty-six years of pain

When I was around eight years old, I became best friends with three school-mates. We remained best friends through high school and university.

After university my life was not going well. I had a falling-out with one of my best friends and we drifted apart. I was at fault for this breakup, but at the time I blamed her.

I was stuck in a bad relationship and could not find a good job. Things all around me were unpleasant.

I knew my best friends were doing well: they found good jobs, got married, had children, bought homes. I was jealous of them and did not want to see them when they tried to reach out to me.

Years passed and I had no communication with any of them.

One of these friends went to my parents' house to drop off a note for me to call her, but my stubbornness and closed heart prevented me from doing so.

My life was so bad that I went to many psychics in search of answers as to why this was happening to me. They could not give me answers.

In 2015, when I was fifty years old, I attended a workshop with Master Sha in Vancouver and started to attend classes and workshops at the Master Sha Centre Vancouver, where I learned about the importance of forgiveness practice. It was a struggle for me to do the practice initially, but I persisted. Slowly my heart opened more and more. My life started getting better.

Then, in the summer of 2015, one of my former best friends stopped by my parents' house and my sister happened to be visiting at the same time. The friend told my sister that she really missed me and wanted to see me. When my sister told me this, I was still hesitant to call my friend. I felt so embarrassed at how I treated her and our other friends and did not think I could face them.

I started including these friends in my forgiveness practice every day for two weeks. Then one day, I decided to email this friend to apologize for what I did. She was very gracious and accepted my apology.

She gave me the email addresses of the other two friends. I emailed both of them to apologize. They were both very loving and forgave me.

We decided to get together before Christmas. We had not seen each other for twenty-six years. When we finally saw each other, we started crying. It was very emotional for me to think that I wasted all these years with these

wonderful women because of my petti-
ness and jealousies.

We had a wonderful time together
catching up. It was like old times. Now
we make an effort to see each other at
least once or twice a year.

I am so grateful for the wisdom and
practice of forgiveness. I know that forgiveness has brought these friends back
into my life.

Yvonne L.
Vancouver, British Columbia

Immeasurable relief and gratitude

My most vivid and instructive forgiveness experience came some years before
I met Master Sha, or even learned about
Ho'oponopono, a Hawaiian practice of
reconciliation and forgiveness, which

was my first real instruction on the practice of forgiveness.

At the time, my husband and I were working as construction contractors, I as a house painter and restorer. I had done several weeks of work for a client and friend, only to find out that he was going to pay me only about half of what the work was worth.

I was angry and hurt, and there seemed no recourse to what I saw as being cheated out of my income. It was like an ulcer or a cold sore. I worried about it and fussed and fumed for weeks.

One day as I was walking my dogs in a park near our home, I encountered this client on the path. We just stood and looked at each other for a time, then all of a sudden, I said, "I forgive you." I hadn't meant to say it; it just came out of my mouth. He threw his arms around me, saying, "Thank you! God bless you. God bless you."

I felt this huge wash of relief, light, love, and releasing that started at my feet and flooded up through me. It was the most amazing feeling of freedom and sweetness!

I have never forgotten that moment or that feeling, and I incorporate it in my forgiveness practices now, telling those whose forgiveness I am requesting about the great relief and gratitude that comes from forgiving.

Kristin
Highlands Ranch, Colorado

Everything shifted with ten minutes of practice

When I met Master Sha, I had already practiced forgiveness for thirty years, and it certainly helped keep my life *smooth. What is different about Master Sha's approach is the simplicity and targeted goal for the specific outcome.*

I experienced a situation that caused so much pain that I could not even stand to be under the same roof with the individual. Due to my targeted forgiveness practice of ten minutes with the key people involved, everything shifted and opened my ability to cope with the situation. As a practicing acupuncturist, I now use this approach for clients who are ready to heal their emotional pain.

I am forever grateful for learning these very important steps and the ability to self-clear shen qi jing blockages for a smoother journey through life.

Our world is suffering; forgiveness practice can help set us free.

H. L. Albers, M.Ac., L.Ac.
Locust Grove, Virginia

~ ~ ~

Forgiveness is not an occasional act.
It is a permanent attitude.
—Martin Luther King Jr.

~ ~ ~

Finances

Long-overdue accounts paid in full

I have many miraculous stories from forgiveness practice, and I am so happy to share two of them.

When I joined a dental manufacturing company in 2009, I was employed as accounts manager and was looking after their accounts and credit control. They had several clients who had not paid for several years. It was my task to collect old debts.

There was one client who had not paid for four years. I started calling him and sending letters, some of which were demanding and threatening, and there was still no response for eighteen months. Then I met some Master Teachers of Tao Academy in 2011, learned about forgiveness practice, and knew how powerful it could be. I did forgiveness practice with this client for a few weeks. Out of the blue, he phoned to say that he owed the company some money and wanted our bank details. The next day the money was in our account. Not only that, he overpaid us! With the forgiveness practice I did not have to ring the client at all! This was a miracle.

My second story is with the same employer. Another client did not want to pay what she owed for repairing her dental x-ray machine.

I chased payment for about three months. I did forgiveness practice for a few weeks. Then I called her to request the outstanding amount. She was very nasty and said a few rude words. I told her I forgive her and I love her. She was speechless! The money was in our account ten minutes later. Another miracle story!

Harsha G.
London, England

Daily forgiveness practice brings massive changes

Since I was introduced to Master Sha's teachings in 2018, I've been doing the forgiveness practice from his Greatest Love book along with tracing either the Da Ai (Greatest Love) or Da Chang

Sheng (*Greatest Flourishing*) *Tao Calligraphy* cards. *I try my best to do forgiveness practice and calligraphy tracing for a minimum of thirty minutes every day.*

Through these practices, I've been able to transform my negative mindsets around money and finances. For my entire adult life, I have suffered from fear, anguish, and disappointment around my lack of finances. Over the past couple of months, I am seeing shifts in how financial opportunities are presenting themselves to me. I no longer have negative mind chatter. I'm not at all afraid of or gripped by the thought of money, or what could happen if I don't have enough of it. I am grounded and peaceful, knowing I am on a path of transforming this area of my life. Once this massive change took place, many areas of my life began to shift positively.

I am very grateful for this powerful and effective life-changing practice that provides me with a daily foundation for living my life.

Sandra B.
Vancouver, British Columbia

Forgiveness brings desired job

I was suffering severe financial difficulties in October 2017. My income was low.

I was looking for a job with a reputed company. I had worked for this company earlier in my career, but I left for another job.

I started doing a forgiveness practice by writing forgiveness letters, offering forgiveness, and requesting forgiveness from the soul of the company and all *souls related to that company. I did this every day for two to three weeks.*

In November 2017, I got a call for an interview with the company. I cleared the interview, and by the last week of November I was working again for that company. The best part was, the week I joined the company, they had organized a family day for all employees. I was able to take my wife, Amruta, and four-year-old son, Kaveesh, to my new company and they were so happy about it. Kaveesh was thrilled to visit his father's workplace. After that my finances improved a lot and were more consistent.

Forgiveness practice is the greatest treasure to humanity.

Sachin Medhi
Pune, India

~ ~ ~

Forgiveness is not always easy. At times, it feels more painful than the wound we suffered, to forgive the one that inflicted it. And yet, there is no peace without forgiveness.
—Marianne Williamson

~ ~ ~

Work

One forgiveness practice transforms a work relationship

For months, the director of my department often seemed stressed or frustrated. One day, as we began to work together to train a few practice managers, we had a falling-out, which made for a rather uncomfortable work environment for everyone in the department associated with us. We agreed to disagree on the issues and left it at that.

Three months later, I did the forgiveness practice in the Greatest Love book. I sought forgiveness for the lack of harmony and for any unpleasant hurt created by me or my ancestors, and kindly suggested to the director's soul that we communicate to voice our concerns in a manner both of us would understand better.

Three days after my forgiveness practice, the director asked me to chat with her privately about something not related to our department. In the meeting, she apologized for her unpleasant behavior over the last few months. She even highlighted the areas where she had seen me improve and emphasized the positive impact on the department of the work I was doing. The compliments were well thought out and delivered in a *manner that was sincere, genuine, and kind.*

When I left that meeting, I felt like I had communicated with a completely different person. We both showed respect, kindness, and an affinity for each other's efforts.

I am so grateful for forgiveness practice. It allowed us to reconnect and be of service to each other in a hectic environment with constant changes.

Edward A.
San Francisco, California

No workplace drama!

A few years ago, I was in a very stressful work situation. I was teaching full-time at a college, and apart from my boss and me, there was only one other full-time instructor in the program. My boss's position as program coordinator was up for a vote, and my only other full-time colleague decided to run.

She had often complained to me about our boss in private, and my boss had often criticized her flaws to me, again, in private. Neither of them liked each other. But since both of them were running for the election, that left me with the deciding vote! Whoever won (and lost) the election would know whom I voted for, and it would be a very unpleasant work environment with that person afterward. What a dilemma!

I consulted one of the Master Teachers of Tao Academy, who did a spiritual reading that gave me insight into the situation. She also guided me to do sincere forgiveness practice.

I did forgiveness practice sincerely every evening. After three days, my *colleague (the other full-time instructor) withdrew from the election! The forgiveness practice had removed the soul blockages, and the physical world drama was totally avoided.*

Hardeep Kharbanda
Hawaii

Forgiveness transforms workplace aggression

I was attracted to Master Sha's teachings because they are based on love and the power of one's soul to change one's life and the lives of loved ones. I have had tremendous healing through Master Sha's practical wisdom teachings.

Today I would like to share an experience I had about five years ago. I was working with a person who was hurt by one of my actions. This person became very angry with me and began bullying me at every turn. At the time, I felt my only option was to go to my supervisor to seek resolution. When my coworker found out that I had gone to our supervisor, she became even angrier and insisted that the three of us meet at the end of the week. I told her that I would communicate with her but needed the weekend to think through what had happened. She was not happy with my decision to wait, saying that I was putting her off.

Over the weekend, I did forgiveness practice. Although I really didn't know what I had done to make this person so angry, I still asked for forgiveness from her soul and told her that I loved her. I communicated to her soul that I wanted us to have a good working relationship and that I would do my best to contribute to our team in a positive way.

The day of our meeting with our supervisor, I arrived five minutes early. I continued to chant and remained peaceful and calm. When we met, I was shocked by my coworker's behavior. She began to sob and apologized for how poorly she had treated me. I remember that I didn't speak the entire meeting.

We continue to work in the same profession and see each other often. Life is so much easier when people can work together in a loving and positive way.

I have used the forgiveness practice many times since and have found it to be the most helpful way to transform situations that seem hopeless.

J. Noyce
Virginia

~ ~ ~

To err is human; to forgive, divine.
—Alexander Pope

~ ~ ~

Life Transformation

Look within for deeper forgiveness and compassion

This is a forgiveness story that I will never forget and that I hold as a great example of selflessness and service.

One of my clients shared this story with me some years ago. She was hiking the trail to the famous Machu Picchu citadel in Peru with a small group of students and a Buddhist monk. Suddenly a man came up from behind and grabbed the monk's shoulder bag, which contained his wallet, identification, and several other personal items. The man turned and started running down the mountain. The monk started running after him and shouting for him to stop. The students followed suit and also ran after the man, shouting at him to drop the bag, upset that this man had the nerve to steal from their teacher for whom they held such reverence.

After quite a chase, the monk was the first to catch up with the man. The students soon followed and started to chastise the man for stealing from the monk. Feeling ashamed, the man immediately handed the bag over to the monk. The monk said to him, "Sir, I just want you to know that it's okay. Whatever I did to you, I am sorry." The monk then handed the bag back to the man and said, "Please take whatever you need. I forgive you. We are free." The man stood in shock, *not sure how to respond, but grateful. The students stood speechless, not knowing what to say or do but feeling an even greater reverence for their teacher.*

This story taught me that whatever happens in my life that may seem like a challenge can be a great opportunity for deeper forgiveness and compassion. It shows me that I can consider the impact on another when I feel hurt or taken advantage of. I can ask myself what are we exchanging in this seemingly negative entanglement, and what would be the best way to transform it instantly?

I'm grateful for all of the lessons learned and for the example of others who have shared their wisdom and understanding so that I may grow on this life journey. Forgiveness has most certainly brought me inner peace and inner joy.

Sher O'Rourke
Toronto, Ontario

Nearly homeless, forgiveness transforms everything

In 2016 I was leading a healing group at a shelter for women at risk of homelessness. One of them came to me one day and asked for help. She was living at the shelter due to a marriage breakdown after being abused by her husband. She had no family or support system in Australia and was unemployed.

For eighteen months, she was involved in numerous court hearings with her husband, who would not agree to a settlement. She was sure that he would continue to place obstacles in her life and felt there was no solution to the situation.

I suggested that forgiving him could help transform the situation. Her immediate response was a strong, "No, why should I forgive him? He is the cause of all my problems." We spoke about the pain of the anger, resentment, blame, and more that was contributing to her suffering and unhappiness. She agreed with the teaching of unconditional forgiveness and decided she was willing to give it a go.

We did a practice of asking for forgiveness from and offering forgiveness to her husband. We requested support from Heaven and connected to the Tao Calligraphy Da Kuan Shu in the Soul Healing Miracles[7] book. For about fifteen minutes, we chanted "Da Kuan Shu" and "greatest forgiveness" while visualizing light in her heart. She felt very peaceful and happy afterward.

I gave her the book and asked her to continue this process with the Tao

---

[7] *Soul Healing Miracles: Ancient and New Sacred Wisdom, Knowledge, and Practical Techniques for Healing the Spiritual, Mental, Emotional, and Physical Bodies*, Dallas, Texas/Richmond Hill, ON: BenBella Books/Heaven's Library Publication Corp., 2013.

Calligraphy for at least ten minutes each day.

In a few weeks, she came back to the shelter and joyfully explained that everything in her life had changed. She had been back to court and, miraculously, her husband settled without question. She also shared that, the day after we did the first forgiveness practice, someone gave her two hundred dollars after seeing her request for support on the internet. She said she had been requesting money through many avenues for months, but this was the first time anyone responded. She mentioned being gifted a sewing machine. To top it off, not long afterward she was offered permanent accommodation and was able to move out of the shelter.

I saw her some months later and she shared that she chants "Da Kuan Shu" often and was positive that forgiveness practice was the catalyst for all the positive changes in her life. She was very grateful for discovering the power of forgiveness and Tao Calligraphy.

Leonie Lawrence
Melbourne, Australia

Forgiveness brings oneness

In the summer of 2016, I was chanting the heart song Love, Peace and Harmony one day. While singing the second line, "I love all humanity," I heard the words, "even Daniel." I was surprised to hear these words, as I had done forgiveness practice many times with this person.

Earlier that year, my son was in a terrible car accident. He was trapped inside the vehicle for about forty-five minutes. The emergency responders stated that it was the most difficult extraction they had ever done. My son was airlifted to the nearest hospital. He underwent two surgeries and was in a wheelchair for six weeks. It was life-changing for our family. Daniel was the driver who caused the accident.

After hearing Heaven's guidance, I immediately started doing forgiveness practice with Daniel's soul. I went deeper and deeper within my heart during this time. I had many great breakthroughs in my own life.

A few months later, my son, daughter, and I went to Daniel's sentencing. The atmosphere in the courtroom was tense and clearly divided. Everyone had lost something in the accident: the mother grieving the loss of her transitioned daughter; the grandparents care-taking the toddler whose mom could no longer function due to trauma from the accident; the young children whose father was now facing many years in prison along with his own mother and father grieving the loss of their son. The pain of everyone involved was palpable.

In a sentencing hearing, victims can speak to the judge and address the person being sentenced. I decided to share what I had learned over the past few months through my forgiveness practice. After saying a few words to the judge, I turned to Daniel and said, "Someone once told me that forgiveness brings inner joy and inner peace. I choose this today. I forgive you. I hold nothing against you."

In that moment, Daniel started sobbing. His family gasped in relief. The tension in the courtroom softened. Hearts opened. Even the mother who lost her daughter asked the judge if she could say a few more words. She expressed to Daniel that she would work toward *forgiving him. It would take time, but she was committed to it.*

Shortly after this, the judge called a recess to determine Daniel's sentence. It was during this time that I witnessed miracles. The aisle that separated the two sides was bridged. Hugs and tears were exchanged. It was one of the most moving moments of my life.

Forgiveness is the most powerful tool that I have experienced in my life. I am grateful for the message I heard that day. If I hadn't gone deeper into my own heart, finding peace with the situation and truly letting go, I wouldn't have been able to share the words of Master Sha: forgiveness brings inner joy and inner peace— words that broke hearts open, allowed compassion to seep in, and brought forth oneness where division once was.

Kristina Darling
Denver, Colorado

Forgiveness brings
happiness and twins!

When I first met Master Teachers of Tao Academy, I was seeking healing for my fertility challenge. My husband and I tried almost everything to overcome this challenge. I so wanted to be a mother and make my husband a happy father.

As I started to learn more and do the practices, my heart started to open further for deeper healing. After two years, I was able to open my heart fully to forgiveness. Now I can humbly and with infinite gratitude share that I am a beyond-words-happy mother, nursing infant twins. There are not enough words or space in any book to express our deepest gratitude for all the healing techniques and practices.

I forgave myself for any negative shen qi jing blockages related to pregnancy a month before we conceived our beautiful twins. I also offered forgiveness to all those who had offended me.

Forgiveness has changed our lives forever—mine, my husband's, my whole family's, and all those who meet our happy babies.

Monica Castro Gartner
Alberta, Canada

Generations have been empowered

When I had my first child, I had just ended a difficult relationship. I was single, in high school, and living well below the poverty line. I had a lot of anger toward my child's father, my father, and my father's father for the line of single mothers they left to raise their children alone.

My anger was affecting me deeply. I was upset that I was one of many single mothers in my family and did not want the same for my daughter. My greatest fear was that my anger with these men would negatively affect my daughter. I have heard spiritual teachings that your respect for God, a deity, or your spiritual teachers is connected with your respect for your parents. I hoped that my daughter would respect her father deeply so she could hold peace in her heart. Out of my desire for her happiness, I became determined to heal my relationship with her father and my father.

Through my spiritual studies, I concluded that the family patterns I was upset with were in fact my family's karmic lessons. This did not make those experiences punishments but rather gifts of teaching to help us grow into the strong, loving people our souls desire us to be. *Forgiveness practice is a powerful tool for receiving the loving essence and teaching from your painful experiences.*

For days, weeks, and months I did deep forgiveness practice with her father, my father, and myself. The forgiveness practice model also emphasizes service and creating love, peace, and harmony. Knowing that, I nurtured the desire in my heart to help others and applied it to these men in my life. My prayers cried out for their blessings, their success, their health, and their happiness to come to fruition, regardless of the suffering I felt they had caused me. It was an empowering lesson for me. Instead of blaming them for my struggles, I owned my own experience and embraced the lessons as an act of God's love for me. My difficult memories with them could no longer fuel my anger.

Through forgiveness practice, I am now able to tell my four-year-old daughter only the beautiful stories about her father. My heart forgave and developed love for our fathers, so I can share that love with her. As for the fear I once had of her repeating the same family pattern of single motherhood, I know that love melts blockages. Her being surrounded by unconditional love is the best way I can empower her to have the most beautiful life possible. Because of this wisdom and healing experience gained from doing forgiveness practice, several generations in my family have been empowered to heal and grow in the deepest of ways.

Kayla Darling
Denver, Colorado

Conclusion

Everyone and everything is made of shen qi jing. Shen includes soul, heart, and mind. Qi is energy. Jing is matter. Soul is the content of the message. Heart is the receiver of the message. Mind is the processor of the message. Energy is the actioner. Matter is the transformer.

How does everyone and everything in countless planets, stars, galaxies, and universes work?

How does all life, including health, relationships, finances, and more, work?

They all work through the following process:

Soul leads the heart. Heart leads the mind. Mind leads the energy. Energy leads the matter.

Why do people get sick? Why do people have relationship challenges? Why do people have financial and business challenges? Why do people have challenges in every aspect of life? All challenges are due to negative shen qi jing. Negative shen qi jing is disorder, disconnection, and disharmony.

To transform all life challenges, transform negative shen qi jing to positive shen qi jing.

Soul is the ultimate boss of a human being. Soul is the ultimate boss of everyone and everything. Soul blockages are the root blockages in every aspect of life. In Tao Science, we call soul blockages *negative information*.

To transform soul blockages is to remove the root blockages in order to transform all life.

Greatest forgiveness—unconditional forgiveness—is sacred wisdom and practice to transform all kinds of soul blockages. It can also transform negative shen qi jing to positive shen qi jing.

Therefore, forgiveness is the sacred key to unlock your blockages to transform all life.

Practicing with the Tao Calligraphy *Da Kuan Shu* (figure 1) can boost and accelerate this transformation beyond comprehension. Use the techniques revealed in this book to transform your health, relationships, finances, and every aspect of life.

I forgive you unconditionally.

You forgive me unconditionally.

Bring love, peace, and harmony.

Transform. Transform. Transform.

I love my heart and soul
I love all humanity
Join hearts and souls together
Love, peace, and harmony
Love, peace, and harmony

About the Authors

Dr. and Master Zhi Gang Sha is a world-renowned healer, Tao Grandmaster, philanthropist, humanitarian, and creator of Tao Calligraphy. He is the founder of Soul Mind Body Medicine and an eleven-time *New York Times* best-selling author. An MD in China and a doctor of traditional Chinese medicine in China and Canada, Master Sha is the founder of Tao Academy and the Love Peace Harmony Foundation, which is dedicated to helping families worldwide create happier and healthier lives. A grandmaster of many ancient disciplines, including tai chi, qigong, kung fu, feng shui, and the *I Ching,* Master Sha was named Qigong Master of the Year at the Fifth World Congress on Qigong. In 2006 he was honored with the prestigious Martin Luther King Jr. Commemorative Commission Award for his humanitarian efforts, and in

2016 Master Sha received rare and prestigious appointments as Shu Fa Jia (National Chinese Calligrapher Master) and Yan Jiu Yuan (Honorable Researcher Professor), the highest titles a Chinese calligrapher can receive, by the State Ethnic Academy of Painting in China.

Master Cynthia Deveraux is a Certified Master Teacher of Tao Academy and Master Sha's only lineage holder. As one of Master Sha's authority teachers, Master Cynthia has traveled the world alongside Master Sha for eleven years, offering powerful healing and compassionate guidance to thousands.

Master Cynthia has always had a deep spiritual connection to the Divine. From the age of three, Master Cynthia was guided by the message that there needs to be a deep awakening and opening of our hearts and souls in order for Earth and humanity to survive.

For twelve years before meeting Master Sha, Master Cynthia pursued an intense daily meditation and forgiveness practice. Her personal experience with sincere forgiveness helps anyone in Master Cynthia's presence experience a feeling of deep peace and healing.

Devoted to helping humanity live in love, peace, and harmony, Master Cynthia is completely aligned with Master Sha's teachings of ancient and modern wisdom and spiritual practices.

Master David Lusch is a Certified Master Teacher of Tao Academy. He has assisted in the training of thousands of Tao Hands Practitioners, Soul Teachers, Soul Communicators, and Master Teachers worldwide.

As one of seven authority Tao Teachers to spread Master Sha's highest teaching and wisdom, Master David offers secret and sacred wisdom, practices, and healing blessings.

When he met Master Sha in 2004, Master David had suffered from obsessive-compulsive disorder (OCD) for most of his life. Searching for self-healing techniques, he dedicatedly learned Master Sha's system, received healing blessings, and practiced daily. Within one year of meeting Master Sha, Master David was completely healed of OCD and, working with his psychiatrist, halted all medication, which he had expected to take for the rest of his life.

As the author of *How I Healed My Obsessive-Compulsive Disorder*, Master David shares his soul healing experience to inspire and give hope to others who are suffering from "incurable" conditions.

Selected Other Books by Dr. and Master Sha

Soul Mind Body Medicine: A Complete Soul Healing System for Optimum Health and Vitality. New World Library, 2006.

What is the real secret to healing and transformation? World-renowned healer Dr. and Master Zhi Gang Sha gives us a simple yet powerful answer to this age-old question:

Heal the soul first; then healing of the mind and body will follow.®

In *Soul Mind Body Medicine*, Dr. and Master Sha shows that love and forgiveness are the golden keys to soul healing. From that foundation, he presents practical tools to heal and transform soul, mind, and body. The techniques and the underlying theories are easy to learn and practice and profoundly effective. They include:

- Self-healing methods for more than one hundred conditions, from the common cold to back pain to heart disease to diabetes
- Step-by-step approaches to weight loss, recovery from chronic illness, emotional balance, and maintenance of good health
- A revolutionary one-minute healing technique

The Power of Soul: The Way to Heal, Rejuvenate, Transform, and Enlighten All Life. Heaven's Library/ Atria, 2009. Also available as an audiobook and a trade paperback.

The Power of Soul empowers you to understand, develop, and apply the power of soul for healing, prevention of sickness, rejuvenation, transformation of every aspect of life (including relationships and finances), and soul enlightenment. It also empowers you to develop soul wisdom and soul intelligence, and to apply Soul Orders for healing and transformation of every aspect of life.

This book includes a bonus *Soul Song for Rejuvenation* mp3 download as a gift to every reader.

Soul Healing Miracles: Ancient and New Sacred Wisdom, Knowledge, and Practical Techniques for Healing the Spiritual, Mental, Emotional, and Physical Bodies. Heaven's Library/BenBella Books, 2013. Also available as an audiobook.

Millions of people on Mother Earth are suffering from sicknesses in their spiritual, mental, emotional, and physical bodies.

Millions of people have limited or no access to health care. They want solutions.

Soul Healing Miracles teaches and empowers humanity to create soul healing miracles. Readers learn sacred wisdom and apply practical techniques. This book includes nine calligraphies written by Master Sha. Everyone can create his or her own soul healing miracles.

Greatest Love: Unblock Your Life in 30 Minutes a Day with the Power of Unconditional Love. Heaven's Library/ BenBella Books, 2017.

Feel the greatest love. Experience the greatest love. Embody the greatest love.

We all have challenges that keep us from experiencing this greatest love—unconditional love. These challenges may present themselves in your health, relationships, or finances. With this book, learn how to unblock your life in 30 minutes a day with the power of *unconditional* love, the greatest love, which surpasses human love and enters the love of all creation.

The power of greatest love can melt all blockages and harmonize all separation and all that is not love. Carry this treasure with you to apply its wisdom anywhere, anytime, to enrich and bless your health, relationships, finances, intelligence, and every aspect of life.